Finding Water,
Holding Stone

Also by James Bertolino

Volumes

Pocket Animals, 2002
Snail River, 1995
First Credo, 1986
Precinct Kali & The Gertrude Spicer Story, 1982
New & Selected Poems, 1978
The Alleged Conception, 1976
The Gestures, 1975
Making Space For Our Living, 1975
Employed, 1972

Chapbooks

Bar Exams, 2004
Pub Proceedings, 2001
26 Poems From Snail River, 2000
Greatest Hits: 1965-2000
Goat-Footed Turtle, 1996
Like A Planet, 1993
21 Poems From First Credo, 1990
Are You Tough Enough for the Eighties?, 1979
Terminal Placebos, 1975
Soft Rock, 1973
Edging Through, 1972
Becoming Human, 1970
Stone-Marrow, 1969
Ceremony, 1968
Drool, 1968
Day of Change, 1968

Finding Water, Holding Stone

Poems by James Bertolino

Cherry Grove Collections

Published by Cherry Grove Collections
P.O. Box 541106
Cincinnati, OH 45254-1106

Typeset in Palatino by WordTech Communications LLC,
Cincinnati, OH

ISBN: 9781934999554
LCCN: 2009927432

Poetry Editor: Kevin Walzer
Business Editor: Lori Jareo

Visit us on the web at www.cherry-grove.com

Acknowledgements

We gratefully acknowledge the editors of the following magazines and anthologies where many of these poems first appeared—sometimes as earlier versions: *Bellingham Review, Beloit Poetry Journal, Chrysalis, The Cortland Review, Crab Creek Review, The Drunken Boat, Every Other Weekly, Fireweed, Gargoyle, Jeopardy, Journal of Contemporary Anglo-Scandinavian Poetry, Manzanita Quarterly, Notre Dame Review, Pavement Saw, Ploughshares, PoetryMagazine.com, Pontoon, Portland Oregonian, Raven Chronicles, Solo, StringTown, Switched-on Gutenberg, The Temple* and the anthologies *Fresh Water*, edited by Jennifer Bosveld; *Orbis: 100 Major Modern Poets*, edited by Mike Shields; *Parnassus of World Poets*, edited by Ramasamy Devaraj; *Quarterly Review of Literature: 50th Anniversary Anthology*, edited by Theodore and Renee Weiss; *The Talking of Hands*, edited by Robert Alexander, C.W. Truesdale and Mark Vinz; *Urban Nature*, edited by Laure-Anne Bosselaar; and *The Writer's Journal*, edited by Sheila Bender. The poems "Touch the Blues" and "Wisdom" were published in the chapbook *Greatest Hits: 1965-2000*, Pudding House Publications.

Renowned butterfly expert Robert Michael Pyle has identified the lovely creature on the cover of this book as *Campaea perlata*, the Pale Beauty—an inchworm or looper of the family *Geometridae*.

For my mother, Doris Robbins Bertolino, at 90

Contents

One: Finding Water

The Path of Water 13
Blueprint 14
Molecules 15
You May Believe 16
Ice 17
The Mystery 18
Turn 19
Three Crows 21
A Triumph 22
Sun Worship 23
Out of Step 25
Sequoia 26
The Baying 27
The Liquid Dark 28
What Water Says 29

Two: Declensions of Love

That Sunday 33
Smiling Down 34
Broken 35
Wisdom 36
Touch the Blues 37
Return to Manzanita 39
To Make Mud 40
Split the Sun 41
Her Breath 42
Detritus 43
What Abides 44
Lupine 45
Untamed 46

The Rapture..47
Like Taut Persimmon 48

Three: Having Stone
Having Stone 51
Flares...52
Bloodying August Polito's Nose...........53
Chowder's Last Day...............................54
The Rescue 56
A Picnic Scene..57
Distracted 58
No Fear 59
In the Kitchen...60
Stew...61
Absence..62
The Lost: A Fractal Pantoum.................63
His Disorder..64
Terminal Routines..................................66
My Cathedral 67
Black Hills National Cemetery..............68
Children of Rioters.................................69
Like a Toy..70
Smudged Window 71
The Blouses 72

One: Finding Water

The Path of Water

Nothing can make water better. —Ursula LeGuin

Water builds.
Water waits.
Water grows heavy
with its own wounding.
Earth is the planet of water.
We are water. We are the history
of water in this star system. We sip
molecules that brought oxygen to the tissues
of blind fish. Our breaths remember ice.
Sweat remembers clouds sliced by pterodactyls
on leathery wings. Water rises and sinks.
Water that traveled by comet for thousands of years
finds news of the universe in the urine
of Tibetan priests. Water teaches.
Water is the path that takes us
in. We swim
the mind of water.

Blueprint

This morning the ice came.
Everything fresh
and new—but don't be fooled.

Water is old.

When it's just cold enough,
ice will enclose everything—pebbles,
twigs, ripe fruit and all
we've built—in a brilliant casing.

This is the way water memorizes
what is temporary and
in danger. Water carries the blueprint
for what has been made,

what is missing.

At this moment, in the profound depths
of the Pacific, water is remembering
a perfect model of Hiroshima
in April of 1944.

It is glowing with the pink
of plum blossoms.

Molecules

Back when electric lights
were a new thing,
people thought the tiny

flashes they sometimes
saw beyond the corners
of their eyes

had to do with
the mystery of electricity.
Now we know those

blinking bursts are from
almost unimaginably small
alien spacecraft.

We needed to comprehend
that intelligence doesn't reside only
in things that are large.

Even molecules have
creation myths
to help prove

they exist.

You May Believe

A facet of beach sand
makes its way to the sea.
Given the particular shape

and weight, I notice how original
the dance it enacts, within
the sometimes steady,

sometimes fickle forces
of the receding water.
At one moment of its course

a tiny item of debris catches
and holds the flicker, until an
increasing sweep of current

allows it to spin free.
If I needed confirmation,
I could follow this

cogent drama to where
the incessant waves will at last
remove all semblance of purpose.

You, my special friend,
may believe your life
is different from that small body

of sand, but I do not.

Ice

At a distance we saw a sapling with an
encrustation

of ice or snow.

Closer, where the bark
had split away, in an area
at eye-level and above, the moisture
fanned out into a long

frill of lacy

crystals, as though the soul
had needed to leave, but was frozen
in an ephemeral gesture,
temperature

too low perhaps

for death to complete
its arduous project.

The Mystery

I remember the sound of redwing
blackbirds lacing

the humid air over the swamp.
Picking my way down the pump-house trail

in high-topped sneakers, I paused
at a break in the trees and looked out over

the marshy lowlands, fetid acres
that were a brown that moved, that seemed

to undulate like the skin of an enormous snake.
When I ran the rest of the path and leaped, I sank

ankle-deep in a frothy mud, an ocean of baby toads—
none of them larger than a dime.

I felt that expanse of life pulling at my stomach,
weakening my knees, and knew then

the world is a mystery of excess, which will never
recede from its love of death.

Turn

Being quiet with a wren
    whose busy chatter
        has quit
and whose shining eye

blinks at me, head swiveling
    above a few grams
        of feather and
delicate bone, heart the size

of a ripe currant in
    rhythmic detonation: I breathe
        and the chip, chip,
chitter resumes.

Being quiet with the architecture
    of a fungus, guarding
        its moisture on a dead snag excavated
by woodpeckers—

the complex ridges and lines
    are the contours
        of an old face, which holds
the expression of that moment when

defeat gains the depth
    of a lesson learned.
        Then my mind is silenced
by forest gone beyond

pattern: the pleasure
    of finding sense

is illusion,
and I am again alone in a world

that does not care. I turn
and start for home.

Three Crows

I walk with Stella, my dog, the four-legged, blue-eyed
avatar, beneath the cliffs of Kelly's Point,
where thousands of years of tropical mud
ooze clear liquid above us.

To the West, heavy clouds seem to smother
the islands, with glowing chinks edging
them red. A spirited breeze brings salt,
and Stella lopes toward the surf where three crows

have been exchanging opinions over their rocks.
They lift, twist playfully into the easy wind, then swoop
down to tease her—coming within inches
of her tall ears, her jaws. She leaps and hovers

like Nijinsky, head turning to track the black wings.
Again. Again. When the crows climb out of their game
to crest the cliff behind us, Stella runs in circles
like a mad thing, onto the beach and

back to the water, elated by the crow magic
bestowed on her. I notice then a change over
the horizon: the molten cracks in the clouds
have widened to blast furnaces.

I feel the heat on my face and know
it's what I've needed, what I've come for.
I let that power fill me, nod, then turn
with Stella to go on.

A Triumph

A mind just roared by
on a motorcycle,

leaving a flash
in my retina.

I have noticed
the way the setting sun

will select a single window
in the foothills and,

from a distance of miles,
that shining seems greater

than all else. At evening
the Great Blue Herons fly inland

to roost, one after another over
an hour, each making its individual

compromises with the air.
Yet together, their steady

succession is a triumph:
the certainty of light

finding form in
the living.

Sun Worship

Looking like Muslims at prayer, they gather
in rows over the silk
and twig-ridges
of their tents. When the sun
commands, they do a synchronized dance—
weaving side-to-side with a snap
that quickens.

Wearing saffron yellow and
millennial black, they are
the tent caterpillars, and in their millions
an unsavory prey.

Today, we see one march the length
of a bleached log, searching
for the single sacred place where cocooning
feels right. When it pauses, and curls like something
soft
you'd want to touch, my companion explains
if you see a chalky spot that glows
against the dark of the forehead, it means
this supplicant has been chosen
by a wasp who's laid an egg.

Later, inside the cocoon, that humid
rebirthing chamber, it will hatch
and feed greedily on the sacrificial host.
Swollen then with such rich nourishment, such
spiritual fat, the young wasp will poke
a portal through and,

like a moth driven ecstatic
by light, ascend.

Out of Step

A blue caterpillar makes its leggy return
to a silk cloister on the sill.

Below the open window, I stumble
through a dream of love and

rejection—a child again, fallen
out of step with the millipede, my teacher.

Like a cooling mantra, an early morning breeze
ripples, then settles over my tightened brow.

I will honor the thousand-legged,
the single heart.

Sequoia

When fire moves
like a flood and

each smallest breath
is a claim, each sigh

a relinquishing, you ask
what a thousand-year-old Sequoia

has learned of the wind.
What does it desire?

When only the tallest prayers
rise beyond black clouds

blistering the sky, it's time
to embrace what burns.

Spirit confirms what matter knows.

The Baying

The unearthly sound
of the train's horn

gets the hounds baying,
the neighborhood mutts

howling, and I look up to see
in the evening sky

a full moon, voluptuous
and ripe—that unearthly light

stirs the animal
in me: Listen.

The Liquid Dark

How can we forget the womb,
or even less forgettable,
our own births?

Imagine how a bat, flying blind through
a moonless night, makes its way
at great speed between boulders and trees.
What if the echo of its squeaks come to describe
everything as liquid? The massive cliffside
is a waterfall, with broad curtains of spray.
Angling its wings, the bat slips deep into stone, where
its body slows to stasis, and its pulses return
with news of a world as thin
as light.

I said how can we forget the womb?

What Water Says

Leafless aspens groom
the iced breeze, while below

a brook descends the mountain
with its musical story, remembering

the serenity of sky, and lightning's clear passion.
Water knows what is far will be near.

Water says choose that which closes distance,
choose touch. When snow falls

and a green mystery is carried
by all that moves,

choose love.

Two: Declensions of Love

That Sunday

I'm walking under willows, and when
she comes to me, it's with wrens.

Out hanging on the smallest branches I see wings
fluttering. Then feel, as I did once,

her hand like a feather on my neck.
"You've come back to me. You're home!"

But I am mistaken, and have been, and there
will be no wrens. I could have told her

how beautiful she looked with her hair free
and receiving the sunlight that day

in the park. But the sun
has gone.

Smiling Down

For awhile life was better—
the smallest details
were reason for pleasure, her car

starting, a face smiling down
from the billboard advertising
a local savings & loan.

But the old anxiety returned
to its home in her, and its
heavy webbing spread

to snare everything, the way rain
and a good wind will take
any flower's petals down.

She needed a memory,
and returned to the ocean where
his hands were still up under

her new sweater, his fingers
were not cold, yet her nipples
shivered all the way down.

Broken

Theirs is something broken
he would like to fix.

It's just parts, scattered
like scratched bits of metal

and glass, with a few ripe
berries squashed, and a smear

of something that looks like
sunlight on a red dog's

fur. Such is the gathering
he keeps near, but what is broken

stays undone.

Wisdom

"I wake up like a stray dog
  belonging to no one."
      —Jack Gilbert

Some days I don't want wisdom,
don't want art, just need to have someone near
to hear my silences, my large and little

noise. Never asked to be alone.
I'd take something as shallow as affection,
someone to ask me anything. Someone

to love me a chance to answer. I mean give me
a chance to give. A poet I was
wrote that when a love dies you carry

a heavy rock until you can't
anymore, and then mark where
you set it down. This is called

"Carrying the Stone." What a poet does
is carry his mark. I've said we draw nectar
from the fractures but I know

that's a lie. All love is one love
is another. I don't want all love,
I want hers. But I'd take anything

as deep as her hands dipped in my shallows.
If someone touches you are not alone.
Take wisdom. I need someone near.

Touch the Blues

Say I'm a man of 53 years,
flexible in my thinking, yet shaped
by certain heavily reinforced concepts
about my relationship with the world.

Say I'm someone who cannot speak seriously
for long without blurting a phrase,
some winking word-curve that proclaims
I'm ready to ride pleasure
all the way to reverence.

Okay, I'm alone, stepping carefully down
metal stairs to a blues
club above a river in England. It's smoky,
and dark.
              Keeping my eye on the piano player,
because
he's playing brilliantly, and because the small stage
is a source of light,
I fumble blindly
for a table.
              I'm convinced if I look toward the music
I will find my way.
                    Settled then into a chair, I discover
with pleasure I'm not alone here. Her face glows
with the blues.
              A shiver
ripples through
my chest. Despite
a growing intimacy, I begin the usual
mental listing of setbacks
                    until the sax lays down

a moan.

Shaking her head, my stranger

says, "It's okay.
Don't." She moves
her hand,
        her naked skin
toward mine,
              and her voice gives birth
to the kind of phrase
that changes you:
                "Choose this chance
to touch me."

Return to Manzanita

They took their failed love
to the Oregon coast, where

the early February storm
was monstrous and exquisite,
the beach covered four feet deep
with gelatinous foam, winds keening
at gale force and the rain horizontal
in volumes of wet. They kept

to the hill, inside their honeysuckle cottage,
where she built a fire that beckoned
wildly, and seductively, and softly until
it sank into its orange heart.

Then they moved closer, and gave
themselves to be consumed.

To Make Mud

Can I say I want it all, want it now,
want it big and sweet
and twisty, want it small?
I want the scented fur
and good dirt beneath the nails.
Want to be there to wail

when her feral eyes blaze.
I want to touch with my tongue the lines
between her brows, to feel
where the tips of her soul
tingle.

I want the pledge of her, the fledge of her breast
and wings, the talons
of her protective heart. I want to make
mud with her, shape and flow
with her. I want the droplets

of dew festooned
along her cutting edge.
I want the tiny love-bomb
where she folds in.

I want to be her niche, her sack,
her sway-backed beast of love.

Split the Sun

She would split the sun
for him and
count twice
each scale of a salmon

at spawn. She would blow
milkweed pods
to pieces
just to show the breeze

where it's going. And when
the loon begins its
liquid moan,
the heat of her listening

would tip the grasses away
from the moon,
would shape
around them a nest.

Her Breath

She is where the song
sits down and weeps

for joy, where the red-winged
blackbird calls for what comes

after. She is the river
splashing the moon onto darkened stones,

the broken yolk that beckons the sun
to its yellow nest. Her breathing

stitches what time
has torn.

Detritus

Looking away
over the estuary
to the smooth
mid-summer sea,
she told him her heart
was a loose gathering of shards.

He said that fits
the definition of
detritus, where good living things
have their structures collapse,
and become thus
accessible to the hungry.

I am here, he said, to feed
on your heart.

What Abides

As the years go, and you find
your view of the world

to be ever more identified
with history, it is a comfort

to have a field of study, a steady
involvement you return to each day—

something large and enclosing
which time does not transform.

In this way a love, or an abiding
friendship, might grow in value,

might become more true, as all
that promised you permanence

begins to twist and diminish
with the years.

Lupine

It would seem late,
yet darkness waits, and

the wonders attributed
to his name are not all

limited, or small. Evenings like this
he remembers a gift

that traveled years, perhaps
lives, to reach him—well past

the middle of his day. It was
a generosity he'd grieved, then

was given, as when the leggy lupine
brings to high alpine slopes

her intoxicating intervals
of blue.

Untamed

She has fully appeared,
yet he hears wings
and sees light fluttering
at the verge of shape, senses shadows
of yearning.

When she speaks,
his arms become flowering vines
that pull toward a mountain
rising.

An uneven,
untamed thing
could be set down between them,
and there it would be symmetrical, and
of beauty.

The Rapture

When need shivers on the brink
of knowledge, she turns her ear

toward Andromeda. All around her
the pond peepers and crickets, the shrill

piping of the velvet-winged, are enclosed
by her singing. Her song is the rapture

that begins with moss licking feet and ends
in the stars. Far beyond the celestial

curtain, Shiva has heard those small
silky notes and, taking hold

by her hair, pulls her through
to the other world.

Like Taut Persimmon

Come, lie down
where your hair may yearn
into the earth, where fear
is the last garment you fling.

Columbine and rain, azalea
and sunrise,
the world reaches
with two hands, two wings
over the hills.

Rest for a feathered moment
over the depths, then ease
your long-limbed spirit beyond
limitation. Stand naked
in the river of arrival.

Now wave to someone you love.

Like ripe pear, like taut
persimmon,
you fill
with mystical sugars.

Three: Having Stone

Having Stone

There's a story that the Samurai
would test a new sword by slicing
a criminal's body in half.

One doomed man was said
to have quipped: "Wish I had
swallowed a stone for my breakfast!"

Having stone at the heart is expecting
the sword, is wanting that brief
satisfaction in blunting an edge.

Flares

Some part of me is in prison.
One of my gestures was, then wasn't,

then was a bullet. I feel like I've become
a card in the Tarot deck, but nothing

major. And there are rumors
going—I know them as a slight

irritation, the taste in my throat
that signals sickness.

Sun flares make the world strange.
Something is changing shape,

and I've heard it's my heart.

Bloodying August Polito's Nose

I was a freshman in high school, a "minim"
at St. Bede Academy, and for no good reason
bloodied August Polito's nose.
It felt like a lump of pink clay to my fist.
He staggered back, then stood there, eyes wide
and blinking, while two thick streams of blood oozed
down his lip. I was satisfied to have hurt someone
I knew wouldn't hit me. I remember

the Summer I was fifteen and killed
a snapping turtle. The entire shell was buried
in the sandy shore of a shallow river
I'd waded through. Only the head protruded,
and when I stepped too close, those ferocious jaws
lunged and snapped. They missed my bare foot,
but in retaliation I swung my hatchet again
and again, creating a bloody stew.

Only after I pulled the ruined carcass free,
to survey my passionate work, did I see fat yellow eggs
the size of marbles. I gasped, crouched
alone there with my shame. The same
shame I should have felt for the evil
I'd done to the soft, egg-shaped Polito,
who with his raw complexion and
thick-lipped smile wanted only
to be my friend.

Chowder's Last Day

The neighborhood veterinarian said
she'd die, and soon, of Feline
Leukemia. Her father's name was Elvis,
and she'd lived with a brood of show cats
in an Idaho double-wide filled
with Presley memorabilia.

As a kitten she had ears that resembled oysters
in a creamy bisque, so he named her Chowder.
"I'll take her home for the weekend, to say
goodbye," he said. The doctor cocked his head,
then nodded. She was gaunt, her muscles
almost gone, eyes glowing blue crystals.

That night he brought her to bed to snuggle, though
she seemed uncomfortable as she folded and
settled lightly on his chest. He petted just the fur
of her and drifted off. Later, he awoke suddenly
from a confusing dream to hot liquid on his skin
and the sharp odor of urine. In spontaneous
reaction he flung her off him to the floor, then
switched on the bedside reading lamp.

Just inside the fuzzy circle of illumination, she
crouched where she'd landed on the hardwood, holding
an awkward position. Her body shivered, eyes turned blankly
toward the dark. He picked her carefully up,
took her to his damp body. She felt clammy, an alien
thing, more dead than living.

After making her a bed of soft towel,

and getting himself clean, he returned to an uneasy
sleep.

When finally the hesitant light of Winter
began opening the bedroom,
he rose and searched for Chowder, who'd left
the upstairs, was not on the first floor and had,
no doubt in great pain, made her way
to the basement. He found her there
in the shadows, licking slowly
the cold concrete floor.

The Rescue

I went up the hill
the day you
left here, and rescued the gopher snake.
I put a heavy glove on my right hand
and brought a pillowcase.

I also lifted a small green frog
out of the cave
for good measure, though she
was likely the only creature not trapped—
they have sticky fingers.

The lizards were fat and happy:
their supply of black beetles
seems endless. Also, there was something
I found disturbing. Another mouse
had fallen down, and the insects were making
a slow meal of it. The way

it lay, inert, accepting, sometimes jerking
in understated agony, became
an image of how
our lives can be.

A Picnic Scene

Lift the wine while history
fogs you in.
There's Dolores,
wearing her First Communion whites, undies
in pink—just thirteen months
before the accident. And young Jesse—
why does Jesse appear? Trying to warn her
with his hands?

Red blossoms, their sensual recesses;
the black dog with spotted tongue; a sequence
of striped worms perforating the landscape.
And hovering above, something feathered
casts an omen over the scene.

Arranged there, on muted cloth,
is the usual yellow china, and ripe fruit
which, catching the low sunlight, serves as center
for a gathering whose friendly postures
prove there are no masks.

Behind it all foliage is busy
practicing its fractal variations, sometimes
hiding, sometimes revealing
the splendid, unsheathed
talons.

Distracted

Today something fell
inside me, I heard it crash.

For a moment I'd been distracted
by the intimacy between

autumn and sunset,
and let go. I don't know

now what I'll do, because
there's an ambush happening

and I've got to save what I can
of who I am.

No Fear

When you see the crab
moving sideways

in the shadows, you should know
its glossy shell not only protects,

but imprisons. When finally it wrenches
its swelling flesh free, it is flayed

by pain, naked to every least abrasion,
each bite. But the crab doesn't fear

its life is finished. It soon feels itself loose
and lengthened, skin hardening

to new armor. Finds itself grown
more grand, commanding and

fiercely hungry.

In the Kitchen

Before she looked up from the phone,
he overheard her say something
that sounded like *best dancer.*

As he approached, her face shifted
to an uncomfortable grin.

Then she turned away, bending slightly,
as though suddenly sick, and put the phone firmly
into its cradle.

"Does this have anything to do
with me," he asked, brow furrowed.
She whirled and spat the word "no!"
like a bite of rotten fruit.

"You only care about yourself," she sobbed,
hands rising to cover her mouth.

He knew then he'd be going to the diner
for dinner.

Stew

1.

Before he knew
cancer
was snaking its dark
increments through his brain,
he started wearing lace
gloves, so delicate,
so white.

2.

For some, being happy
is like trying to stand on
one foot—of course you can,
but only for awhile: that other
shadowed foot, the foot of frustration
and melancholy, grows heavier,
heavier, and always
goes down.

3.

She has strewn
the remnants
of their stew over
his papers, lumps of rutabaga
and carrot sullying
the syntax
of power.

Absence

"Where could my heart find refuge
from itself? Where could I go yet leave
myself behind?" —St. Augustine

He wants to say this plainly, to howl
over his losses, the holes in his life.

He dug forward as a mole for years, blind
to the dark clotted soil before him, unaware

of the humid emptiness he left behind.
Then he hit granite. When he turned,

there was no path, no well-lit passage
to guide him back. He was afraid

the world he'd stepped through and over
was gone. It was as though he'd been a glutton

who gorged on the granular and real,
then left a trail of lumpy absence.

Now he moans like a stifled infant,
head bald and wet.

The Lost: A Fractal Pantoum

Dial 1-800-The-Lost.
Do it now.
You don't understand where you are.
Don't know who you've been.

Do it now.
You see something in the windows, something dark.
You wonder where you've been and
everyone avoids your eyes.

You see something in the windows.
Coins for the phone are all you ask.
Everyone avoids you.
Nobody cares about your past.

Coins for the phone, but who to call?
When did you begin to feel this way?
Nobody cares if you have a past.
"I know you," is what you need someone to say.

When did your abandonment begin?
You don't remember how you got this far.
If only someone would touch your hand.
Dial 1-800-The-Lost.

His Disorder

When his disorder became known,
it endeared him to the community.
It was thought to be genetic and, in retrospect,
the lineage was clear: he'd come from a long
queue of men who could love only
the smallest things.

They'd fought wars and butchered
calves, but were helpless
to do harm to anything of less stature
than a chipmunk. There would be no murdering
of locusts or earwigs, no indiscriminate flattening
of varmints on the highways.

One troubled year, driving West
through Minnesota, the tires intersected
a salamander migration—thousands of tender-tailed
creatures covered the concrete. Suddenly his hands
were paralyzed at the wheel. His wife took control
while he, in the back seat, covered his ears,
buried his eyes.

To love his family, his children, he must consider them
one limb, one organ at a time: for a freckled nose,
he feels emotion rise; for an entire face, there is nothing.
They've learned to tickle him with a finger,
brush his neck with a curl.

There are stories now that superior beings
have been visiting our planet, and some of us
are afraid, but he knows he will not mind
when they find him—so long as they reach

with something slim, touch his heavy body
one part at a time.

Terminal Routines

The youngest man on Death Row
has your eyes. He tells The Press
you awakened in him a passion
for artichoke.

The Family Doctor makes a joke
out of telling your adolescent daughter
she has cancer. No wonder sunlight
always starts you screaming.

The illumination changes and,
from the empty middle of the room,
you hear a voice saying, "This is your last
chance to listen to me."

Everyone you've ever been believes
in omens. Everywhere you go, mute
children make signs, and your invisible friend
has chosen suicide

again. You close your eyes and leap
into a new love, twisting the pleasure
of sensual space, bare ankles attached
to the taut snap of a blue bungee.

So high in your body
the air is chilling and thin.
Next morning inside the flesh
of your arm, you find a complete bird

imprisoned.

My Cathedral

Were I a woman,
I'd have a thing

to do: an architect, I'd be
on God's business.

The high somber space
inside my cathedral

would be shaped of the silence
that comes only when a dying child

has finished
screaming.

Black Hills National Cemetery

As cemeteries go, this
is a great one to mow.
The stones are evenly planted

(we call them monuments)

and but for holidays, you hardly ever
have folks in your way.

Back during the last war
more people visited, mostly the type
that always brought flowers fresh.

It's the plastic kind I like.
They never wilt
or turn black.

These Fall days are slow, and
the few evenings I work
past daylight, I can hear the soldiers
moaning

when I shut the mower
down.

Children of Rioters

Today we honor the children
of rioters, now grown
fine-boned and slim.

They feel empathy
for what does not survive.

The children of rioters taste cheese
gathered from the milk
of uncontaminated goats.

They have no children of their own.
They will have none.

The children of rioters are geniuses
of time passing with no trace.

Like a Toy

Life seems dimmed
by wants unsatisfied.

No wonder Buddha said desire
is the source of pain.

But like a toy that breaks
into song when a rough cord is drawn

through it, we do find music
in what abrades.

Smudged Window

Pets died, lucrative positions
dried up, those who
professed love
sent their vouchers and

now he's back!

Like a smudged window cleared
with a forearm, the light
breaking in makes the chilled bourbon
a chalice-of-trembling.

He does not pause for the mewling
in the alleyway, does not praise
the bus arriving on time.
These do not matter because

he is owned by a force
unknown, and finds himself
happy.

The Blouses

Just the late afternoon light
dimly stroking

the park—no man of affection
would be satisfied with
so hesitant an approach. Then briefly

the clouds open their white blouses,
and the grass, the flowering
bushes say yes, yes, that's better,

that's what we've needed
all day!

James Bertolino grew up in Wisconsin and his work has been appearing internationally in books, magazines and anthologies for over 40 years. Bertolino's poetry has been recognized nationally by the Book-of-the-Month Club Poetry Fellowship, the Discovery Award, a Hart Crane publication award, a National Endowment for the Arts fellowship, two Quarterly Review of Literature book awards and, in 2007, the Jeanne Lohmann Poetry Prize for Washington State Poets. His books have been issued by such publishers as Copper Canyon Press, Carnegie Mellon University Press, New Rivers Press, Ithaca House and the QRL Award Series at Princeton University. Two of his out-of-print books have been reprinted online by the Connecticut College Contemporary American Poetry Archive. He has served as poetry editor for *Epoch*, and founding editor of *Abraxas* magazine and press, as well as *Cincinnati Poetry Review*. For over 20 years he published books by poets under the Stone Marrow Press imprint. He holds an MFA from Cornell University and taught creative writing at Cornell, Washington State, University of Cincinnati and Western Washington University. For the 2005-06 academic year he was Writer-in-Residence and Hallie Ford Chair of Creative Writing at Willamette University in Oregon. He has since retired and lives on five rural acres with Anita K. Boyle near Bellingham, Washington.

Printed in the United States
221772BV00001B/19/P

9 781934 999554